Please visit our website, www.garethstevens.com. For a free color catalog of all our high-quality books, call toll free 1-800-542-2595 or fax 1-877-542-2596.

Library of Congress Cataloging-in-Publication Data

Sabatino, Michael.
Being an orangutan / by Michael Sabatino.
  p. cm. — (Can you imagine?)
Includes index.
ISBN 978-1-4824-3283-1 (pbk.)
ISBN 978-1-4824-3284-8 (6-pack)
ISBN 978-1-4824-0137-0 (library binding)
1. Orangutan — Juvenile literature. I. Title.
QL737.P96 S23 2014
599.883—dc23

First Edition

Published in 2014 by
Gareth Stevens Publishing
111 East 14th Street, Suite 349
New York, NY 10003

Copyright © 2014 Gareth Stevens Publishing

Designer: Katelyn E. Reynolds
Editor: Therese Shea

Photo credits: Cover, p. 1 Dane Jorgensen/Shutterstock.com; cover, pp. 1–32 (background texture) AnnabelleaDesigns/Shutterstock.com; pp. 4–5, 9, 14 iStockphoto/Thinkstock.com; p. 7 (inset map) pavalena/Shutterstock.com; p. 7 (main) Tuomas Lehtinen/Shutterstock.com; p. 8 Eric Isselee/Shutterstock.com; p. 11 Khoroshunova Olga/Shutterstock.com; p. 13 (inset) Marko5/Shutterstock.com; p. 13 (main) Christian Kober/Robert Harding World Imagery/Getty Images; p. 15 MJI007/Flickr/Getty Images; p. 17 Fuse/Thinkstock.com; p. 19 Anup Shah/The Image Bank/Getty Images; p. 21 Jan S./Shutterstock.com; p. 23 A & J/Iconica/Getty Images; p. 25 Rodney Brindamour/National Geographic/Getty Images; p. 27 Romeo Gacad/AFP/Getty Images; p. 29 Art Wolfe/Stone/Getty Images.

Printed in the United States of America

CPSIA compliance information: Batch #CW14GS: For further information contact Gareth Stevens, New York, New York at 1-800-542-2595.

CONTENTS

Words in the glossary appear in **bold** type the first time they are used in the text.

WILD IMAGINATION

Do you ever wonder what it would be like to live in trees high up off the ground? You could get around by swinging from one branch to the next. Each day when you woke up, you'd search for fruit to eat. Each night before you went to sleep, you'd make your own bed using leafy branches.

You've just imagined a day in the life of an orangutan! Read on to find out more about these primates that live up in the trees.

imagine that!

Orangutans are a kind of ape. They're the only apes covered with red hair.

Primates are a group of **mammals** that include monkeys, apes, and humans.

LEAFY HOMES

If you were an orangutan, you'd live in a rainforest. Rainforests are tall, thick forests that get lots of rain. Over half the world's plant and animal **species** live in rainforests. That's an incredible number, since rainforests cover only about 6 percent of Earth's surface!

The rainforest provides all the food orangutans need to live. They really like the fruit that grows on the rainforest trees, such as figs and mangos. Sometimes, they'll eat leaves, bugs, and even tree bark.

Wild orangutans can only be found on the islands of Borneo and Sumatra in Southeast Asia, shown below.

South China Sea

Borneo

Sumatra

INDIAN OCEAN

7

STARTING OUT

If you were an orangutan, you'd live most of your life high in the rainforest **canopy** of the Southeast Asian islands of Borneo and Sumatra. An orangutan starts its life a lot like a baby human. The mother orangutan gives birth after about 8 1/2 months.

For 2 years, the mother carries her baby wherever she goes and provides all the food and care it needs. As the baby grows, it spends less time clinging to its mother. It gets stronger and starts climbing branches on its own.

A baby orangutan is in constant contact with its mother for the first 2 years of its life.

9

WORKING MOM

A young orangutan will stay with its mother for about 8 years. During that time, the mother teaches her child how to find food and survive in the jungle. Finally, it's ready to live on its own.

After this happens, the mother is ready to have another baby. She'll start all over again and raise another child until it's ready to be on its own, too. A female orangutan may have four or five babies in her lifetime.

Even when they're old enough to find their own food, young orangutans stay close to their mother and often sleep in the same tree.

11

BRANCHING OUT

A grown-up orangutan is well **adapted** to climbing trees. If you were an orangutan, you'd use both your hands and feet to hold on to tree branches. Your long arms would help you reach from branch to branch. You'd be seven times stronger than a human and have no problem lifting yourself up a tree!

Orangutans rarely walk on the ground. They often spend as many as 3 weeks without touching the forest floor! When they do walk, they walk on all fours.

imagine that!

A male orangutan's arms may stretch 7 feet (2.1 m) from fingertip to fingertip!

Orangutan fingers and toes form a natural hook shape, making it easy to hold on to tree limbs and other objects.

13

DIFFERENCES

Male orangutans are larger than female orangutans. They can weigh more than 180 pounds (82 kg) and stand as high as 5 feet (1.5 m). A female orangutan might only be half the size of a male. After male orangutans leave their mother's care, they travel farther from their mother's home range than females.

Female orangutans don't mind being near other females in a territory. They may even eat together. However, males usually avoid each other.

A male orangutan can grow large cheek pads and a throat pouch.

15

UP TO THE CHALLENGE

Sometimes, a male tests a **dominant** male for its territory. A male orangutan may flash its teeth to scare off the **challenger**. The new male might roar loudly and shake tree branches to frighten the dominant male.

If the challenging male wins the fight, it gets to be the dominant male in the territory. That means it can **mate** with the females living in the area. If the challenger loses, it could be greatly injured by the dominant male—or even killed!

imagine that!

Male orangutans may have staring matches to challenge each other, too!

If you were an orangutan, you'd spend a lot of time by yourself. Orangutans spend more time by themselves than other kinds of apes.

17

CALLING HOME

Male orangutans can roar and growl for minutes on end. These sounds are named long calls. Orangutans make long calls for several reasons. Calls may draw females, mark territory, warn off other males, and signal others that it's time to move to another location for food.

When they're annoyed, orangutans make a squeaking, kissing sound with their lips. Sometimes, they puff out their throat pouches. Can you imagine doing these things to show you're unhappy?

An orangutan's long call can last up to 4 minutes!

19

THE HIGH LIFE

If you were an orangutan, you'd begin your day in the morning searching for and eating food for a few hours. After your morning meal, you'd spend the middle of the day resting. Does that sound like a nice day to you so far?

When late afternoon came around, you'd travel around your home range, looking for more food sources and a place to rest at night. An orangutan usually covers about a half mile (800 m) in a single day's travel.

imagine that!

Orangutans have prehensile feet, which means their feet can be used for grasping or holding, like a hand.

Orangutans eat many kinds of plants but are mainly frugivores. That means they mostly eat fruit.

21

NEST REST

When their busy day of eating and traveling is over, orangutans get pretty tired. As each night approaches, they make nests in the forest trees using leafy branches. They sleep in their nests all night long—up to 14 hours!

Studies of orangutan nest building show just how smart these primates are. They use thick branches at the bottom of the nest to support their weight. Then they put smaller branches on top to make a kind of soft **mattress**. Can you imagine building your bed each night?

imagine that!

Scientists think orangutans may choose nest locations for comfort more than for safety from predators.

Nest building can take 30 minutes. An orangutan tests its nest to make sure it will hold its weight.

23

TOOLS FOR THE JOB

Getting to tasty bugs that live inside trees and plants is tricky. If you were an orangutan, you'd use tools! Orangutans have learned how to use sticks to **forage** for bugs as well as to get at seeds inside fruit. They've been known to use leafy branches as flyswatters, too!

Orangutans are some of the smartest primates around. When faced with a problem, an orangutan takes its time and thinks about it before trying possible answers.

imagine that!

Some orangutans are fishermen. They've been seen using simple wood sticks to jab at fish in ponds!

Orangutans use tools to help them survive in the rainforest.

25

ENDANGERED

Orangutans have to watch out for tigers, leopards, and crocodiles, which are their main predators. However, people are their biggest threat today.

Orangutans' rainforest **habitats** have been growing smaller because of human activity. Logging, forest fires, and road building have shrunk their living area. People illegally hunt orangutans for their meat or to keep them from eating their crops. Young orangutans are sometimes sold as pets. Because of all these threats, both Bornean and Sumatran orangutans are **endangered**.

Much of the orangutan rainforests have been cleared for palm oil plantations. Palm oil has many uses, such as in foods and fuels.

PALM OIL KILLS

C🦧P
Centre for Orangutan Protection
www.cop.or.id

HANGING ON

The Bornean orangutan population has decreased by over 50 percent in the last 60 years. The Sumatran orangutan population has decreased by 80 percent over the last 75 years. It's considered **critically** endangered.

Organizations have been created to help orangutans. Some help injured or orphaned orangutans. National parks have been created to set aside habitats for orangutans. Is it enough? After imagining life as an orangutan, don't you think we should make sure these amazing animals are around for a long time to come?

Scientists' best guess, or estimate, is that there are just over 60,000 orangutans left in the wild.

Orangutans in the Wild

species	estimated number remaining
Sumatran orangutan	7,300
Bornean orangutan	54,000

GLOSSARY

adapted: changed to suit conditions

canopy: the uppermost spreading branchy layer of a forest

challenger: one who invites another into a contest or fight

critically: seriously

dominant: the most powerful or strongest

endangered: in danger of dying out

forage: to go from place to place looking for food

habitat: the natural place where an animal or plant lives

mammal: a warm-blooded animal that has a backbone and hair, breathes air, and feeds milk to its young

mate: to come together to make babies

mattress: a large pad on which to sleep

species: a group of plants or animals that are all of the same kind

FOR MORE INFORMATION

Books

Bredeson, Carmen. *Orangutans Up Close*. Berkeley Heights, NJ: Enslow Elementary, 2009.

Ganeri, Anita. *Orangutan*. Chicago, IL: Heinemann Library, 2011.

Newman, Aline Alexander. *Ape Escapes! And More True Stories of Animals Behaving Badly*. Washington, DC: National Geographic Society, 2012.

Websites

Orangutan
kids.sandiegozoo.org/animals/mammals/orangutan
Read more about orangutans and watch them at the zoo!

Orangutans
kids.nationalgeographic.com/kids/animals/creaturefeature/orangutan/
Check out more fun facts about orangutans.

INDEX